SHAKA

KING OF THE ZULUS

D I A N E S T A N L E Y

A N D

P E T E R V E N N E M A

Illustrated by

D I A N E S T A N L E Y

MORROW JUNIOR BOOKS / NEW YORK

For Catherine and Ame Vennema,
with affection

Printed in the United States of America.   1 2 3 4 5 6 7 8 9 10
Library of Congress Cataloging-in-Publication Data
Stanley, Diane. Shaka, king of the Zulus/by Diane Stanley and Peter Vennema; illustrated by Diane Stanley.   p.   cm.
Summary: A biography of the powerful nineteenth-century military genius and Zulu chief.
ISBN 0-688-07342-5. ISBN 0-688-07343-3 (lib. bdg.) 1. Chaka, Zulu Chief, 1787?–1828—Juvenile literature.
2. Zulus—Kings and rulers—Biography—Juvenile literature. 3. Zulus—History. [1. Chaka, Zulu Chief, 1787?–1828.
2. Zulus–Biography.] I. Vennema, Peter. II. Title. DT878.Z9C565 1988   968.04'092'4—dc19
[B]   [92]   87-27376   CIP   AC

PRONUNCIATION GUIDE
(in order of appearance)

Shaka (oo-Shá-geh)

Senzagakona (Sen-zah-gah-kó-nuh)

kraal (kráhl)

Bulawayo (Bul-ah-whý-oh)

lobola (lo-bó-luh)

Nandi (Náhn-dee)

Madlatule (Mah-shla-tóo-lay)

assegai (ah-seh-gái)

Dingiswayo (Din-gis-whý-oh)

Zwide (Zwée-day)

Ndwandwe (N-dwáhn-dway)

Gqokli (Qó-kli)

Dingane (Din-gá-nyeh)

Once there was a little boy named Shaka, who would one day grow up to be a legendary king. He was born in 1787, the son of Senzagakona, chief of the tiny Zulu clan. The Zulus were not important or powerful. They were one clan among many whose kraals, or villages, dotted the hillsides of southern Africa. Shaka's kraal was called Bulawayo.

At the age of six, Shaka became a working member of the clan. Like all young boys, he had to watch the cattle, sheep, and goats as they grazed on the hillside.

Herding cattle was boring work, but it was very important. These animals meant everything to Shaka's people. Not only did the Zulus eat the meat and drink the milk from the cattle, they used their hides for clothing. A man could not even get married until he had cattle of his own to pay the lobola, or bride-price, to the bride's family. If a herdboy let something happen to the cattle he was guarding, it was a terrible disgrace.

And that was just what happened to Shaka. It was only a sheep, killed by a wild dog, but his father was still very angry. It might have ended with a scolding, though, if it hadn't been for Shaka's mother, Nandi. She took Shaka's side, something the chief's other three wives would never do. The chief did not like the way she talked back to him. He became so angry that he ordered her to leave Bulawayo and return to her own clan. Of course, her family would have to give back the lobola of cattle. Nandi would be shamed in front of all the people she had known from childhood. And she would have no man to stand up for her and her son.

For Shaka, living with Nandi's clan was like a bad dream. The other boys teased him, calling him a coward and playing cruel jokes on him. They scattered his cattle when he was herding and broke the little clay cows he made.

His only comfort was his beautiful mother. At night she would hold him gently and tell him not to worry, that someday he would be the greatest chief in the land. It didn't seem to Shaka that it could really happen, since he was a poor and fatherless outcast. But in his heart he

believed it, because his mother said so.

It was hard not having friends, but at least he had a home. Then months went by without rain, and he lost even that. They called the drought Madlatule, which means "eat what you can and say nothing." Grain and corn withered in the fields. The cattle found only sparse, dead grass to graze on, and many died. The milk was poor. Shaka and Nandi were too great a burden to the clan, and once again they had to pack up their few belongings and leave.

At last they found a home with another clan where a kindly man gave Nandi protection. Here, Shaka grew up among friends. He dreamed of becoming a mighty warrior and worked so hard at throwing his spear, or assegai, that he became expert at it.

By the time he was fifteen, he had grown very tall and strong. The other boys admired him so much that they chose him as the leader of their age group. But Shaka had never forgotten the cruel words of his boyhood. He felt he could never be happy until he proved that he was not a coward. His chance came very soon.

While he was watching the cattle one day, he noticed that they seemed restless, as if they sensed danger. He listened intently while searching the hillside with his eyes. As he slowly turned, he saw a leopard half-hidden in a tree, hunched down and ready to pounce.

Shaka quickly raised his assegai. Because the weapon could break easily, he had to hold it at the right angle and stand firm against the great weight of the leopard. When it jumped, he was knocked to the ground, but the leopard was dead.

Everyone praised Shaka, and the chief rewarded him. But Shaka's greatest reward was knowing that he could believe in himself again.

Shaka's clan belonged to the empire of a wise and powerful chief named Dingiswayo, known as the Great One. All the boys Shaka's age were soon called to serve in the army of the empire. Each new warrior was given a tall oxhide shield and a handful of assegais.

Shaka and his friends were taught to fight in the traditional way. Each side would run toward the other in a confused mass, shouting threats and insults. When they were close enough, they would throw their assegais. After they had thrown all they had, they picked up those assegais lying on the ground and threw them back. Hardly anyone was ever hurt. The chief, the women, and even the children watched from a nearby hillside, as if it were a sporting event. Finally, one side or the other gave up, threw down their shields, and fled.

Shaka was sure that he could find a better way of fighting than that! For one thing, he hated the idea of throwing his weapon away. He tried using it like a sword, but the head of the assegai was too light, and the shaft was too long and fragile. So Shaka decided to design a new weapon.

He went to the most famous blacksmith in the region, a fearsome man who was said to have magic powers. The Zulus say that the blacksmith recognized Shaka's greatness, even though he came humbly and simply dressed.

"You shall have what you want, Zulu," the blacksmith said, "but it will take time. We will start from the very beginning. I will build a new furnace with new bellows to make sure that the iron is the best. And in your hands this new assegai will always be victorious."

Shaka trembled with joy as he finally held the weapon in his hand, because he knew that the blacksmith had spoken the truth.

Shaka practiced with his new assegai until his movements became as smooth and graceful as those of a dancer. But he always seemed to be bothered by his sandals. They slowed him down and made him clumsy. So he did a daring thing: he began to go barefoot. The countryside was covered with sharp stones and thorns, and at first Shaka was in terrible pain. As his feet grew tougher, his fighting style became swift and sure.

Before long, Shaka had the chance to use his new ways of fighting. The empire was at war. In one of the battles, Shaka volunteered to fight the champion of the enemy in single combat.

As they approached one another, the enemy warrior began throwing his assegais, as usual. Shaka easily stopped them with his shield. Then he rushed forward and used the trick he had been practicing for months: with a swift movement, he hooked the left side of his own shield under the left side of his opponent's, swinging the surprised warrior sharply around. Now the opponent could use neither his assegai to strike nor his shield to protect himself. The death blow was easy.

Warriors on both sides were astonished. It had never happened this way before! Then Shaka single-handedly charged the entire opposing army. When his men recovered from their surprise, they followed him. It was an amazing victory.

Of course, the Great One soon heard about this brash young warrior. He gave Shaka a gift of cattle and honored him as a hero.

Shaka was given more men to lead, and he went on thinking of new ideas. He did not watch from a hillside—he fought along with his soldiers. And he taught them to fight silently, so that they could hear his commands. But the most important thing he taught them was to move together, as one. He made them practice every day, from sunrise to sunset, until they dropped from exhaustion.

Though he was strict with his men, he was generous, too. When he received gifts of cattle from the Great One, he gave most of them to his

best soldiers. And he ordered the older herdboys to march with the army and carry supplies. The men were grateful to be relieved of their burdens, and now they could travel farther to make war.

The Great One did not think of Shaka as a rival. He knew this young warrior was a genius when it came to warfare, so he invited him into his council of advisors. And the Great One made up his mind that when Shaka's father died, Shaka would become the new chief of the Zulus.

Before long, Shaka's father did die, and his half brothers were fighting over who would be the next to rule. Quickly, the Great One sent Shaka, accompanied by a regiment of warriors, to the Zulu kraal.

When all the people were gathered, the spokesman for the Great One said to them: "Children of Zulu! Today I present to you Shaka, son of Senzagakona, son of Jama, descended from Zulu, as your lawful chief. So says the Great One, whose mouth I am. Is there anyone here who does not agree with this decision? If so, let him come forward and speak now, or hereafter be silent."

No one dared to speak.

Then the Great One's soldiers left and Shaka went to work. He didn't have much to start with. The Zulus were a small clan with only

a few warriors. The royal kraal was old and shabby. Besides, the
place reminded him of the miserable days of his childhood.

Shaka began building a magnificent new kraal. He brought in
famous cooks from other clans to teach the Zulus to prepare food the
way he liked it.

And he called up all the Zulu men to serve in the army. There were
only three hundred fifty of them. He divided them into four tiny regiments, each with matching oxhide shields and the new sword-like
assegais. He built a separate kraal for each regiment to live in and
would not allow them to marry until he gave his permission. His
bachelor army fought all the more bravely, hoping to earn the right to
take brides.

Shaka trained his army so well that they could travel fifty miles in a day over rough country. No other army of foot soldiers in history has been able to travel half that distance in a day.

But when Shaka asked his warriors to fight barefoot, they resisted. It was time to establish once and for all who was in command.

He had the parade ground strewn with thorns. Then he showed his men how he could stamp upon them with his tough, hardened feet without feeling pain. He ordered them to do the same. A few men who didn't do it with enough enthusiasm were killed on the spot. After that, the rest stamped with a frenzy until Shaka was satisfied. His point was made. Thereafter, his armies always fought barefoot, and they fought better for it.

Throughout Shaka's life, he ruled through force and fear—that is how he made his soldiers obey him, and that is how his army won battles. It is not an approach that is admired today, as we dream of a world at peace. But Shaka lived in a different age, when nations all over the world went to war to build great empires, believing it was honorable.

As soon as Shaka felt his army was strong enough, he began helping the Great One make war. Whenever Shaka conquered a clan, he brought its young men into his growing army. The women he captured formed his famous female regiments.

Shaka's Zulus had grown large and powerful when, one day, word arrived that the Great One had been killed. His murderer, Chief Zwide of the Ndwandwe clan, now planned to rule the Great One's empire. Shaka stood in his way, so Zwide sent his army to Zululand.

Shaka had only half as many warriors. He couldn't hope to win in a normal battle, but he could choose where to stand and fight, and use every trick he could think of.

He chose Gqokli Hill, which was a good distance from the nearest river and had a hollow at the top. He brought up plenty of food, water, and medical supplies. He stationed his men all around the hill, hiding one regiment in the hollow at the summit. Then he sent a few men to drive the Zulu cattle away in another direction.

As Shaka had hoped, Zwide sent almost a third of his army chasing after the cattle. The remainder attacked up the hill. As they climbed, Zwide's warriors were pressed closer and closer together, until they began to bump into one another, and there was hardly room to lift an assegai. Everything was going according to plan.

The Zulus sat in eerie silence, motionless. Then, at Shaka's command, they stood in one united movement, each warrior stepping forward to stamp with his right foot and beat his shield with his spear. This astonishing display stopped the enemy in their tracks. Then the Zulus began their incredible work with sword and shield. Within minutes, the Ndwandwe had fled down the hill.

When Zwide's tired and thirsty army attacked a second time, Shaka revealed his next trick—for his reserves appeared as if by magic and encircled the enemy.

Zwide escaped with part of his army, but it was a year before he dared to attack the Zulus again. Shaka outwitted him once more, and this time his victory was complete. The empire now belonged to Shaka, and from it he built a nation of Zulus.

In all his life, Shaka had never seen a European. Neither had any of the other Zulus. To the people of Europe, Zululand was a blank spot on the map. But the time came, in 1824, when these two great cultures met face-to-face.

A small band of English settlers had come from their colony at the Cape of Good Hope to trade in ivory. They expected to find the small,

timid clans that lived in other parts of southern Africa. But the first people they met told them otherwise: this land they hoped to colonize belonged to a great king named Shaka, and his power was beyond measure!

One of the Englishmen, Henry Francis Fynn, didn't believe it. He decided to find this Shaka and see for himself. So he headed north, along the beach, in the direction of Shaka's kraal.

Late in the day, he stopped to rest, building a fire and boiling coffee. As he sat quietly, Fynn became aware of a pounding noise, different from the roar of the waves. It grew louder. When he turned around, what he saw took his breath away: a huge column of warriors, running in perfect formation, coming right toward him.

Fynn was terrified. But he decided that it would be safer to stand his ground than to run. The warriors approached him curiously, then stopped.

They couldn't speak the same language, so they used their hands. But Fynn said the name Shaka, and the Zulus understood him. They let him know that Shaka would send for the English when he was ready. Then they turned away and continued on down the beach.

Fynn counted them as they passed. He counted twenty thousand! It seemed impossible to him that an army so large and well-trained could exist without the Europeans' knowing anything about it.

He was thunderstruck when the very next day he met a *second* column of twenty thousand warriors—the other half of Shaka's army, returning from battle.

Before long, Shaka sent a messenger to bring the Englishmen to his kraal.

On this historic occasion, both the Zulus and the English tried very hard to impress each other with their wealth and power. They began by exchanging gifts. Then the Zulus danced. They danced as they fought: ferociously yet with grace, and in perfect unison.

After the dancing was over, Shaka showed his wealth—the royal cattle. One of the herds was driven proudly past the visitors. Fynn, who liked to count, said there were 5,654 of them, each bred to a perfect snow-white.

The English could come up with nothing quite so grand, but they galloped their horses around the kraal, fired their muskets, and shot off some rockets that they had brought for the occasion.

Shaka was kind and friendly to the English. Yet when one of his people did something wrong, he had him killed instantly. The visitors were shocked and told Shaka so. He then asked them how Englishmen punished people who had broken the law. They explained all about jails. Now it was Shaka's turn to be horrified. He thought a swift death was far kinder than being locked up.

The visitors stayed for several weeks. Toward the end of their stay, a terrible thing happened. One of Zwide's spies, who had hidden himself in the crowd, jumped out and stabbed Shaka. The king was carried to his hut, badly wounded.

Fynn had once worked as a surgeon's assistant, and he had some medical supplies with him. He cleaned and bandaged the wound, and gave Shaka what little medicine he had. The wound was very serious. Fynn doubted that Shaka could recover from it. Everyone waited. As the days passed, Zulus poured in from distant kraals. Thousands wept and moaned outside the hut while Shaka lay still, barely breathing. But on the fourth day his fever went down. The king was going to live!

Shaka was deeply grateful to the English. It was the perfect time for them to ask him a favor. And quite a favor it was: they wanted him to sign a paper giving them a large part of Zululand on the coast, so that English traders could settle there. Shaka could not read the paper. He did not think of land as something which could be owned, sold, or given away. He probably meant only to give his permission for them to settle there.

Shaka always considered the English his good friends. It was only later, during the reign of Shaka's half brother Dingane, that the Europeans and the Zulus went to war.

The boy who had once longed for greatness was now a mighty king. Every dream he had shared with his mother had come true. He had even gone beyond those dreams. And yet he was troubled.

He was afraid that he could no longer control his army. It was now too large for him to command alone. He stayed at home and planned the campaigns, but others fought side by side with the soldiers and won their loyalty. The more clans they conquered, the farther away they had to go to fight, and the men were beginning to grumble.

There was something else that troubled him. Shaka had never married, and his mother was the most important person in his life. She

was loyal and loving, his dearest friend. Now, as he saw her growing
old and frail, he began to worry constantly. He couldn't bear the
thought of losing her.

While Shaka was out elephant hunting, a messenger came to him,
saying that Nandi was dying. Heartbroken, he left at once to go to
her. He traveled eighty miles in a day and a night, and arrived only
moments before she died. It was the worst moment of his life. He
sobbed uncontrollably at the terrible loss. And his troubled mind was
pushed to madness by his grief.

Three days later, Nandi was buried. Shaka ordered twelve thousand warriors to guard her grave for a year. Then he laid down the rules of mourning that the whole Zulu nation had to follow. No one was allowed to drink milk; it was all to be poured on the ground after each milking. No one was allowed to plant or cultivate crops. This command was to last for one year, and everyone knew what it meant: mass starvation.

After three months of mourning Nandi, when the food had given out and people were dying, a brave man came forward. He told Shaka to

stop forcing his sorrow on the Zulu people. "This is not the first time someone has died in Zululand," he said. Everyone who heard his words was stunned. Shaka would surely kill this man! But he didn't, for he knew the man was right. The spell of Shaka's misery was broken at last.

Yet he would never be the same again. He said he felt like a wolf out on a flat plain with no place to hide. He didn't seem to care about his people anymore. He slept little, and when he did sleep, he dreamed about death.

The year was 1828, and Shaka did not live to see it end. In the old days, no one would have dared to plot against the king. Now, his two half brothers had no trouble finding help in a plan to kill Shaka, for the Zulu soldiers were angry.

They had just come home from a long campaign. The men expected to return to their kraals for feasting and celebration. Some thought they would be allowed to marry. Instead, Shaka ordered them to march right past their homes, without rest, and head to another war, far to the north. He then made his worst mistake of all: he ordered the older boys, who carried the soldiers' gear, to stay and form a home guard. From now on, his soldiers would have to carry their own supplies. That was the last straw!

The plotters arrived at Shaka's kraal toward evening. They found him alone, admiring his cattle. Just as they were about to strike, visitors arrived, bringing gifts to the king. Shaka welcomed them, and the men sat around talking while the half brothers grew more and more anxious. It would be dark soon. Something was bound to go wrong.

Desperate for the visitors to leave, the assassins decided to frighten them away. One of them rushed forward, shouting at the visitors to stop bothering the king. He waved his assegai and club around angrily. The visitors left quickly. Then, having Shaka alone, they killed him.

They buried him hurriedly, in an unmarked grave. They smoothed the soil over the place so there would be no trace of him.

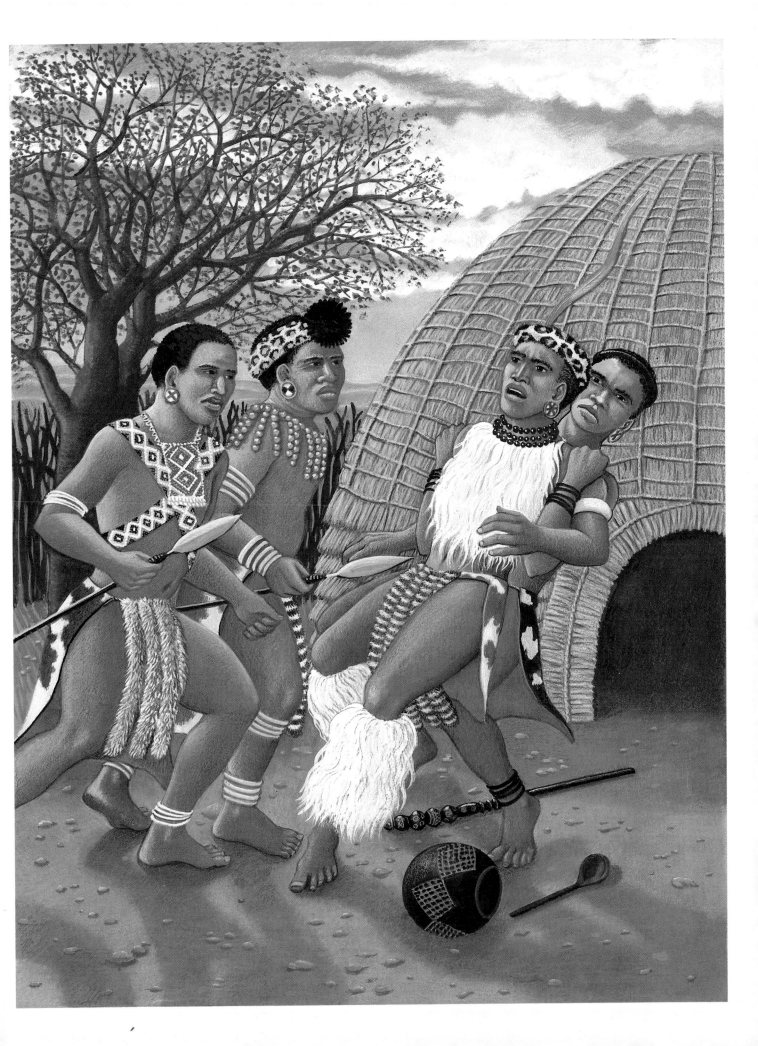

Shaka had been king for little more than ten years, and in that short time he had taken the tiny Zulu clan and built from it a mighty nation. He created an army of the finest warriors in Africa. It was awesome in its power, endurance, and discipline. As a military genius, he has been compared with Napoleon, Julius Caesar, and Alexander the Great. Everything he did, he did boldly and with imagination.

Though Shaka was often cruel, he lived in a cruel age, when wars of conquest were considered glorious and kings held the power of life and death over their subjects.

Today, the descendants of Shaka's Zulus number six million. There are more Zulus in South Africa than any other ethnic group, black or white.

Over the years, they have not forgotten the troubled outcast who became a mighty king. His assassins could hide his grave, but they could not erase his image from the memories of those who knew him. The Englishmen wrote books about him so that men and women who had never set foot in Africa could travel to his kraal in their imaginations. The Zulus told his story to their children, who remembered it all and passed it on, generation after generation.

They still remember it and tell it with pride.

The authors give special thanks to Donald R. Morris for sharing his vast knowledge of Shaka, the Zulus, and the history of South Africa, all of which assisted greatly in the writing of this book.

SOURCES

Bleeker, Sonia. *The Zulu of South Africa: Cattlemen, Farmers, and Warriors.* New York: William Morrow and Co., 1970.

Bryant, A.T. *Olden Times in Zululand and Natal.* London: Longmans, Green and Co., 1929.

*Cohen, Daniel. *Shaka, King of the Zulus.* New York: Doubleday and Co., 1973.

du Buisson, Louis. "The Maligned Monarchs." *Leadership* (Cape Town) 5 (1986): 96.

Elliott, Aubrey. *Sons of Zulu.* London and Johannesburg: William Collins and Sons and Co., 1978.

Fynn, Henry Francis. *The Diary of Henry Francis Fynn.* Edited by James Stuart and D. Mck. Malcolm. Pietermaritzburg, South Africa: Shuter and Shooter, 1950.

Gluckman, Max. "The Rise of a Zulu Empire." *Scientific American,* April 1960, 157–68.

Isaacs, Nathaniel. *Travels and Adventures in Eastern Africa.* Vols. 1 and 2. London: Edward Churton, 1836.

Krige, Eileen Jenson. *The Social System of the Zulus.* Pietermaritzburg, South Africa: Shuter and Shooter, 1936.

McBride, Angus. *The Zulu War.* London: Osprey Publishing, 1976.

*Mack, John. *Zulus.* Morristown, N.J.: Silver Burdett Co., 1981.

Morris, Donald R. *The Washing of the Spears.* New York: Simon and Schuster, 1965.

Ritter, E. A. *Shaka Zulu.* London: Longmans, Green and Co., 1955.

Roberts, Brian. *The Zulu Kings.* New York: Charles Scribner's Sons, 1974.

Tyrrell, Barbara. *Suspicion Is My Name.* Cape Town: T. V. Bulpin, 1971.

Tyrrell, Barbara. *Tribal Peoples of Southern Africa.* Cape Town: Books of Africa (Pty.), 1968.

* These books will be helpful to young readers interested in further research.

DELAGOA BAY

ZULULAND • BULAWAYO (SHAKA'S KRAAL)

CAPE TOWN

ENGLISH ARRIVE 1824